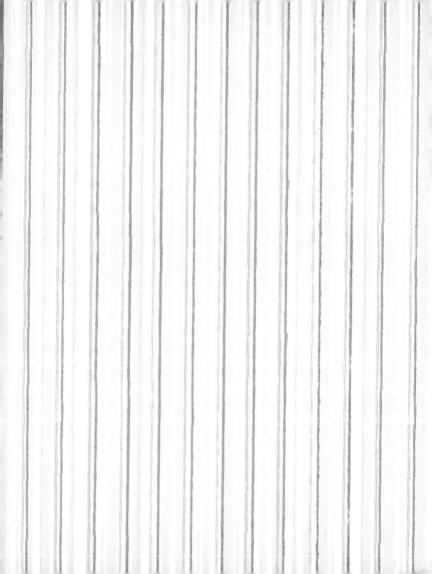

To: _____

From _____

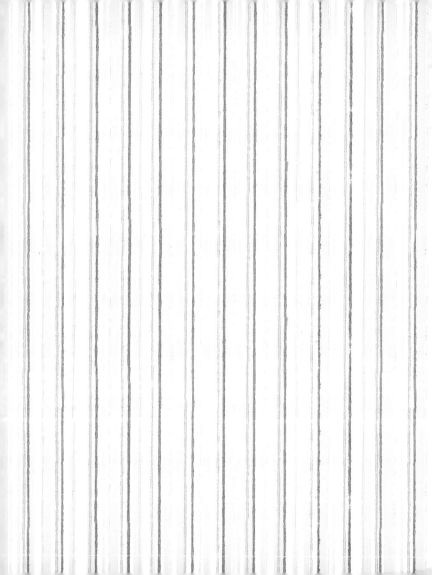

thank you

so much!

CHRIS SHEA

THOMAS NELSON
Since 1798

NASHVILLE   DALLAS   MEXICO CITY   RIO DE JANEIRO   BEIJING

Published in Nashville, Tennessee, by Thomas Nelson. Thomas Nelson is a registered trademark of Thomas Nelson, Inc.

Cover design by David Uttley, The DesignWorks Group and Robin Black, Blackbird Creative. Interior design by Robin Black, Blackbird Creative.

Thomas Nelson, Inc., titles may be purchased in bulk for educational, business, fund-raising, or sales promotional use. For information, please e-mail SpecialMarkets@ThomasNelson.com.

ISBN: 978-1-4041-8789-4

www.thomasnelson.com

Printed and bound in China.

To Lori and Kelly
For whom and to whom
my thanks go on forever...
and dedicated to my
dad,
Bill "Thanks" Givens...

Where do the
unsaid thank you's

go,

thank you's

never spoken

Here you go...

but truly,
    deeply felt?

Thank you's for those
Christmas gifts

and birthday presents

opened long ago;

for books already read
(and thoroughly enjoyed),

candy long since eaten,

a hand-knit
        sweater

worn and worn
and now outgrown,

or a day out
on the ocean

24

in a neighbor's
brand new boat.

Where could they be—

thank you notes for a place
   to call home for a day or
a week or two,

for borrowed cups
of sugar,

or three large eggs
for making
Pancakes,

or a bag of home-grown
    oranges,

a gift left outside
for a Saturday surprise?

Perhaps somewhere

just out of
sight

33

these unsent
    bits
      of
    gratitude

are safely
     tucked
         away,

just never mailed
or
said out loud,

for
reasons

now forgotten...

39

(perhaps it was
  a broken
  crayon,

40

or the perfect
phrase

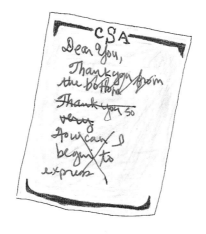

just wouldn't
   come to mind.)

or lack of proper postage.

The truth about
all thank you's

46

Dear Friend,
My heart is filled
with such
gratitude at
your generosity

whether spoken or
written down,

is that they originate
within the heart
  where they stay

  permanently
       recorded,

timeless thoughts of
gratitude
        waiting
          to be said.

So if I've
ever failed
to say
them,

50

& four
profoundly
simple
words,

I'd like to say them, new,

today . . .

52

THANK YOU SO MUCH

53

Thank you for every gift
you've given
me,

54

Thank you for all the
kind things you've done,

56

and thank you most

   a thousand times...

...just
for
being you.